cooking to impress

cooking to impress

TIME
LIFE
BOOKS

Alexandria, Virginia

Time-Life Books is a division of Time Life Inc.

TIME LIFE INC.
Chairman and CEO   Jim Nelson
President and COO   Steven L. Janas

TIME-LIFE TRADE PUBLISHING
Vice President and Publisher   Neil Levin
Senior Director of Acquisitions and Editorial Resources Jennifer Pearce
Director of New Product Development   Carolyn Clark
Director of Marketing   Inger Forland
Director of Trade Sales   Dana Hobson
Director of Custom Publishing   John Lalor
Director of Special Markets   Robert Lombardi
Director of Design   Kate L. McConnell

COOKING TO IMPRESS
Project Manager   Jennie Halfant
Technical Specialist   Monika Lynde

introduction 6

soups & starters 10

Begin a meal with one of these tantalizing dishes, such as Dressed Crab or Thai Shrimp Parcels, and you are guaranteed to have your guests begging for more!

fish & shellfish 28

Fish is a great food to serve the whole year round. It is fast and easy to cook, nutritious, and appealing to the eye, and it tastes superb.

vegetarian 46

Innovative dishes such as Leek Terrine with Walnuts & Feta and Vegetables in Malaysian Coçonut Sauce will tempt even the most stubborn carnivores to eat up all of their greens!

poultry & meat 60

Here you will find classic and modern favorites inspired by flavors from around the world, for when you are out to really impress.

desserts 82

Finish off a feast for friends or family with something sweet and decadent or indulge to your heart's content on delicate fruit. Sugar and spice and everything nice—that's what these desserts are made of!

index 96

contents

6

introduction

Cooking to impress means going to more trouble than usual, spending a bit more time in the kitchen, buying top-quality ingredients and creating a warm and welcoming atmosphere for your guests—putting on a show, in fact. With *Cooking to Impress*, you will be able to create impressive and delicious dishes with ease by following the clear and concise instructions. You may even impress yourself!

Menu Planning

The first step, whether you are planning an intimate meal for two or a large formal dinner party, is to work out your menu, which should be something out of the ordinary and not part of everyday fare. Aim for a balance of color, texture, flavor and variety, and hot and cold food. You don't want fish, for example, in both the main course and the appetizer, or too many dishes that look the same; cauliflower soup, creamy chicken risotto, and homemade vanilla ice cream served on white plates may taste delicious but the overall whiteness can be somewhat bland. Nor do you want too much pastry—not boeuf en croûte and apple pie, or a savory and piquant mousse for an appetizer and a sweet one to end the meal.

Choose your main course first. It could depend on the time of the year—spring lamb at Easter time or game like pheasant or partridge as soon as it comes into season, or perhaps a classic and well-tried favorite such as Burgundy-Style Beef, Sole Bonne Femme, or Duck with Orange. Choose an appetizer that doesn't compete with the main course, but rather works harmoniously with it. A light fish dish such as Seviche of Salmon gets the gastric juices working, while Wild Mushroom Feuilleté has equal appeal to vegetarians and to those with a taste for nature's wild bounty, presented in a sophisticated pastry wrapper. Then think about the dessert. You could consider Red Fruit Salad with Coeurs à la Crème—two treats combined on a single plate—or succumb to the perennial siren song of champagne or chocolate. Both Champagne Summer Berries and Lemon Tart will have your guests coming back for more, as will old favorites such as Chocolate Chip Ice Cream and Chocolate & Cinnamon Bread & Butter Pudding. Finally, don't forget to leave room for a serious piece of indulgence in the shape of homemade Chocolate Truffles, to serve with the coffee and liqueurs.

Next, choose your drinks. Is this to be an informal supper party with a simple choice of red or white wine throughout the meal, or do you want a progression from cocktails and apéritifs, through white and red wines, to a sweet wine with the dessert, and liqueurs with coffee? And, of course, remember to stock up on soft drinks for drivers, and mixers, fruit juices, and spring water, and sparkling mineral water. It is equally important to chill the white wines, to ensure that the red wines have had time to breathe and are at room temperature, and to make sure that you have a plentiful supply of ice cubes.

"The hostess must be like a duck—calm and unruffled on the surface and paddling like hell underneath."

Anonymous

Getting Ahead

One golden rule of entertaining is never to serve any dish that you aren't confident about. If you and your guests are to enjoy your meal, you mustn't make it difficult for yourself. Remember that practice makes perfect so try out new dishes on friends or family, several times, if necessary, before serving them on a special occasion. Another rule is to plan a menu that doesn't involve you spending too much time in the kitchen at the last minute; make as much use of the refrigerator and freezer beforehand as you can. Make detailed shopping lists, do your shopping well ahead, and work out a countdown to make the most sensible and practical use of your time, so that there are no last-minute panics.

Cooking to impress is only one part of the overall picture of entertaining with style. And what this really means is making a social occasion run smoothly, with the addition of a certain amount of panache, to make it go with a swing. Use candles for a softer lighting, select the tablecloth and napkins, polish the silver, clean the glasses, and arrange the flowers, the day before if you can, and then forget all about them.

When it comes to the meal itself, remember that attention to detail shows. Buy the best quality, freshest ingredients that you can afford, make your own mayonnaise, add decorative fruit and vegetable garnishes to your dishes, and choose a really good coffee to make even the end of the meal a treat.

Entertaining is all about adding that little something special and having a good time—so, having made all the preparations, just relax and enjoy!

Decorating Tricks

Cucumber, Orange, and Lemon Slices
To make these classic garnishes look especially decorative, add a fluted edge. Take a 3-inch chunk of cucumber and, holding a lemon stripper firmly, use the notch to remove strips of skin at regular intervals down the cucumber, then cut the cucumber into even slices. Oranges and lemons can be prepared in the same way, and the seeds removed when you slice the fruit.

Frosted Fruit
Small berries and grapes make an excellent decoration for desserts. Wash the fruit carefully and dry it on paper towels, then brush it lightly with beaten egg white and dip it into superfine sugar. Leave it to dry for 15 minutes on wax paper.

mayonnaise

1 Put the egg yolks into a bowl with the vinegar and mustard. Add about ½ teaspoon salt and a generous pinch of pepper, and beat well until you have a smooth paste.

2 Gradually beat in the olive oil, adding it drop by drop to begin with. When the mixture begins to thicken, pour in the oil in a thin steady stream, beating well until all the oil has been incorporated.

3 Or if you prefer, combine the egg yolks, vinegar, and mustard in a food processor or blender, then slowly add the oil through the feeder tube, drop by drop at first, then in a steady stream, until it is all absorbed and the mayonnaise is thick and creamy.

2 egg yolks

1 tablespoon white wine vinegar

1 teaspoons Dijon mustard

1¼ cups olive oil

salt and pepper

Makes about 1½ cups

prosciutto with avocado ●

quail egg tartlets ●

wild mushroom feuilleté ●

seviche of salmon ●

pears wrapped in prosciutto ●

oysters in cream sauce ●

dressed crab ●

crab, asparagus & lemon soup ●

smoked oyster tartlets ●

smoked salmon timbales ●

thai tomato & shrimp broth ●

thai shrimp parcels ●

globe artichokes with garlic & herb mayonnaise ●

soups & starters

1 ripe avocado

6 slices prosciutto, about 3 oz. total

Dressing:

1 tablespoon olive oil

1 teaspoon lemon juice

1 garlic clove, crushed

2 teaspoons chopped parsley

salt and pepper

Serves 2
Preparation time: 10 minutes

1 Cut the avocado in half and remove the pit. Peel off the skin and cut each half into 3 thick slices. Wrap 1 slice of prosciutto around each slice of avocado. Arrange on a serving dish or on individual dishes.

2 Place all the dressing ingredients in a screw-top jar and shake well to mix. To serve, pour the dressing over the avocados.

prosciutto with avocado

■ To preserve the color of cut avocado flesh, rub with a little lemon juice. Handle an avocado carefully as they tend to bruise easily.

1 tablespoon butter

3 sheets of phyllo dough

Filling:

3 quail eggs

3 tablespoons cream cheese

1 tablespoon grated Parmesan cheese

a little cayenne pepper

To Garnish:

chervil sprigs

salad leaves

Serves 2
Preparation time: 15 minutes
Cooking time: 5 minutes

quail egg tartlets

1 Melt the butter and use a little to brush two 3-inch tartlet molds.

2 Place the first sheet of phyllo dough on a board (keep the rest covered with a damp cloth so they do not dry out). Brush with a little melted butter, add the second sheet and brush again, then add the third sheet and brush again. Cut six rounds from the triple thickness, and press into the molds. Bake in a preheated oven, 400°F, for about 5 minutes. Allow to cool.

3 Put the eggs into boiling water and cook for 2 minutes. Allow to cool slightly, then cut in half.

4 Meanwhile, blend the cream cheese and Parmesan, adding a shake of cayenne. Spoon this mixture into the baked phyllo rounds, and top with the egg halves. Sprinkle with more cayenne pepper. Garnish with chervil sprigs and a few salad leaves.

wild mushroom feuilleté

8 oz. frozen puff pastry, defrosted

½ tablespoon butter

2⅓ cups sliced white or cremini mushrooms

1¾ cups sliced oyster mushrooms

⅔ cup sour cream

⅔ cup light cream

1 garlic clove, crushed

salt and pepper

Serves 2
Preparation time: 20 minutes
Cooking time: 10–12 minutes

1 Roll out the pastry to about ¼ inch thick, and cut out three 5-inch circles and three 3-inch ones. Place the circles on a baking sheet and bake in a preheated oven, 450°F, for 10–12 minutes, until puffed up and golden brown.

2 Meanwhile, melt the butter and fry the white or cremini mushrooms for 3 minutes. Add the oyster mushrooms and cook for 2 minutes or until tender. Remove the mushrooms with a slotted spoon, and boil the remaining liquid rapidly until it's reduced to about ½ tablespoon. Add the mushrooms, the sour and light creams, garlic, and salt and pepper. Reheat gently without boiling.

3 To serve, place some mushroom mixture and liquid on top of each large pastry circle. Cover each with a smaller pastry circle and serve.

■ Most supermarkets now carry a large selection of wild mushrooms. Look for porcini, morels, chanterelles, and horse mushrooms as well.

seviche of salmon

1 Cut the salmon fillet into very thin slices—about the same thickness as sliced smoked salmon (lox). Arrange the raw salmon on two plates in a single layer.

2 Sprinkle the salmon with lemon juice and olive oil, and season to taste with salt and pepper. Leave to marinate for a minimum of 30 minutes.

3 Garnish with dill or fennel sprigs, and serve with bread and butter.

6 oz. salmon fillet

lemon juice, for sprinkling

olive oil, for sprinkling

salt and pepper

dill or fennel sprigs, to garnish

brown bread and butter, to serve

Serves 2

Preparation time: 20 minutes plus marinating

pears wrapped in prosciutto

1 Cut each slice of prosciutto in half lengthwise. Cut each pear into 6 wedges and remove the core.

2 Wrap a piece of prosciutto around each pear wedge, and thread 3 wedges onto each skewer.

3 Place the skewers under a preheated hot broiler or on an oiled charcoal grill, and cook for about 2–3 minutes on each side. Serve hot on a bed of salad leaves. Using a potato peeler, shave the Parmesan over the skewers, sprinkle with pepper, and drizzle with a little olive oil.

2 ripe pears

6 slices prosciutto

To Serve:

salad leaves

shavings of Parmesan cheese

pepper

extra-virgin olive oil

Serves 4
Preparation time: 10 minutes
Cooking time: 4–6 minutes

12 fresh oysters in shell, opened, rinsed, and liquor strained and set aside

dry white wine, to fill

Cream Sauce:

2 tablespoons unsalted butter

2 scallions, including green parts, chopped

1 garlic clove, crushed

1 tablespoon flour

¼ cup dry white wine

Tabasco sauce, to taste

1 egg yolk

¼ cup heavy cream

⅓ cup finely chopped button mushrooms

½ cup finely chopped, cooked, peeled shrimp

salt and white pepper

⅓ cup grated Parmesan cheese

2 tablespoons fine dry breadcrumbs

Serves 2
Preparation time: 15 minutes
Cooking time: 30–40 minutes

oysters in cream sauce

1 Measure 1 cup oyster liquor. Add dry white wine to make up the quantity. Scrub the deeper shell halves and add an oyster to each. Arrange in crumpled foil in a pan. Keep cool.

2 Melt the butter in a pan, then add the scallions and garlic. Cook, stirring, until soft but not brown. Stir in the flour and cook for 1 minute, then gradually stir in the oyster liquor and dry white wine. Bring to a boil, lower the heat, and simmer for 15 minutes, stirring constantly. Season to taste with salt and pepper, adding a little Tabasco.

3 Blend the egg yolk and cream. Add 2 tablespoons of the oyster sauce, then stir all into the remaining sauce in the pan. Gently stir until thickened, without boiling. Remove from the heat and stir in the mushrooms and shrimp. Spoon the sauce over the oysters.

4 Mix together the Parmesan and breadcrumbs, and sprinkle over the tops of the oysters. Bake in a preheated oven, 400°F, for 15–20 minutes, or until golden brown and the edges of the oysters begin to curl. Serve hot.

dressed crab

1 Extract the meat from the crab bodies and legs. Tap out the shell of the crab, then wash thoroughly in boiling water, and dry with paper towels.

2 Lightly season the crabmeat with salt and pepper. Separate the yolk and white of the hard-boiled eggs, and push them through a strainer.

3 Mound the crabmeat in each shell, and sprinkle with the lemon juice. Decorate the top with alternating stripes of sieved egg white, chopped parsley, sieved egg yolk, and paprika. Serve each crab on a bed of salad leaves with mayonnaise, lemon wedges, and thin slices of brown bread and butter.

2 cooked crabs, about 1½ lb. each

2 hard-boiled eggs

¼ cup finely chopped flat-leaf parsley

a few drops of lemon juice

paprika

salt and pepper

To Serve:

mixed salad leaves

mayonnaise (see page 9)

lemon wedges

brown bread and butter

Serves 4
Preparation time: 40 minutes

1 Extract the meat from the crabs. Put the shells in a plastic bag and, using a rolling pin, smash them into small pieces. Place the shells in a large pot, with any asparagus trimmings, and cover with 5 cups of the water. Bring to a boil, reduce the heat, and simmer gently for 30 minutes. Strain through a fine strainer into a clean pot.

2 Place the remaining water in a pot with a pinch of salt, bring to a boil, add the asparagus, and simmer for 2–3 minutes until just tender. Drain, reserving the liquid, rinse the asparagus in cold water, drain again, and set aside. Bring the crab stock back to a boil, add the asparagus liquid, reduce the heat, and add the rice. Simmer gently for 12–15 minutes or until the rice is cooked.

3 Place the cream cheese in a bowl with 5 tablespoons of the crabmeat. Season with salt, pepper, and cayenne, and mix well. Toast the bread on both sides until lightly golden. Spread with the crabmeat mixture and keep warm.

4 Reduce the heat under the stock to a minimum. Mix the egg yolks and 2 tablespoons of the lemon juice in a bowl, and whisk in a ladleful of the hot stock. Whisk the egg mixture back into the stock; do not let it boil or it will curdle. Season to taste, adding more lemon juice, if needed. Add the reserved asparagus and the remaining crabmeat, and heat through. Serve at once, sprinkled with the chervil sprigs and accompanied by the crab toasts.

crab, asparagus & lemon soup

1½ lb. crabs, cooked in the shell

½ lb. fine young asparagus, trimmed and cut into 2-inch pieces

1¾ quarts water

½ cup long-grain rice

¼ cup cream cheese

cayenne pepper

8 thin slices of French bread

3 egg yolks

2–4 tablespoons lemon juice

salt and pepper

chervil sprigs, to garnish

Serves 4	
Preparation time: 25 minutes	
Cooking time: 1 hour	

smoked oyster tartlets

1 Roll out the dough thinly and cut into rounds with a 2½-inch cookie cutter. Line 12 greased mini tartlet molds with the pastry rounds, and prick all over with a fork.

2 Blind bake the mini pie shells in a preheated oven, 425°F, for 10 minutes. Remove from the oven and reduce the heat to 375°F.

3 Divide the oysters and parsley among the pie shells. Mix together the egg and cream, and season to taste with cayenne and pepper. Pour the mixture into the pie shells, and bake the tarts for a further 15–20 minutes, or until the filling is set and golden brown.

pastry dough for an 8-inch pie

around 5 smoked oysters, drained and chopped

1 teaspoon chopped parsley

1 egg

⅔ cup light cream

pinch of cayenne pepper

pepper

Makes about 12
Preparation time: 20 minutes
Cooking time: 30 minutes

■ Blind baking is a method of partially baking the pie shell before a filling, which does not need the same amount of baking, or might soak into the uncooked pie shell, is added.

smoked salmon timbales

1 Oil 4 timbale molds. Line them with smoked salmon, and chop any leftover salmon into small pieces. Mix together the taramasalata, cream cheese, Tabasco sauce, lemon juice, and cayenne pepper. Add the chopped leftover salmon. Divide the mixture among the molds. Level the tops and chill well for 2–3 hours.

2 Carefully turn the timbales out of the molds and serve garnished with lemon slices and dill sprigs.

■ If you don't have any timbale molds, baba and dariole molds or small ramekins can be used in the same way.

1 tablespoon vegetable oil, for greasing

6 oz. smoked salmon (lox), thinly sliced

¾ cup taramasalata

¾ cup cream cheese

dash of Tabasco sauce

juice of ½ lemon

pinch of cayenne pepper

To Garnish:

lemon slices

dill sprigs

Serves 4

Preparation time: 15 minutes plus chilling

1 lb. raw tiger shrimp

1 red chile, bruised

3 lemon grass stalks, roughly chopped, or grated zest of 2 lemons

1 tablespoon grated lime zest

4 slices fresh ginger

2 cilantro sprigs

1 quart vegetable stock

2 tablespoons sunflower oil

1 small onion, chopped

2 garlic cloves, sliced

1 teaspoon grated fresh ginger

two 13-oz. cans chopped tomatoes

2 tablespoons light soy sauce

12 basil leaves

Serves 4
Preparation time: 20 minutes
Cooking time: 1 hour

1 Peel the shrimp, set aside the meat, and place the heads and shells in a large, heavy pot. Add the chile, lemon grass or lemon zest, lime zest, sliced ginger, cilantro, and stock. Bring to a boil, cover, and simmer gently for 30 minutes.

2 Heat the oil in a large pan and fry the onion, garlic, and grated ginger for 5 minutes. Add the tomatoes, and simmer for a further 5 minutes. Strain the shrimp shell stock and add it to the tomatoes, along with the soy sauce; bring to a boil, cover, and simmer gently for 10 minutes. Add the shrimp and simmer for a further 5–6 minutes or until cooked. Serve in bowls topped with the basil leaves.

thai tomato & shrimp broth

■ Light soy sauce is generally more salty and used for cooking, whereas the thicker and sweeter dark soy sauce is better for dipping.

thai shrimp parcels

1 Place the garlic, shallot, ginger, lemon grass, lime zest, red pepper flakes, chile oil, fish sauce, lime juice, and sugar in a food processor or blender, and grind to a thick paste. Add the coconut milk and mix well.

2 Place the shrimp in a bowl, and add the coconut spice mixture. Stir to coat the shrimp evenly. Tear off 4 large pieces of wax paper. Place 6 shrimp and a quarter of the coconut mixture in the center of each piece. Wrap up to enclose the shrimp, forming neat parcels. Steam the shrimp parcels over a pan of boiling water for 8–10 minutes.

3 To serve, unwrap the shrimp and place them on plates lined with pieces of banana leaf, if you like. Pour the coconut mixture into a bowl and whisk briefly until smooth. Pour a little over each portion, and garnish with scallions and red pepper strips.

2 garlic cloves

1 shallot, chopped

2-inch piece fresh ginger, peeled and chopped

1 lemon grass stalk, finely chopped

2 teaspoons grated lime zest

1 teaspoon crushed red pepper flakes

2 teaspoons chile oil

1 tablespoon fish sauce (nam pla)

1 tablespoon lime juice

¼ teaspoon sugar

⅓ cup coconut milk

24 raw shrimp, peeled and deveined, tails left intact

To Garnish:

banana leaves

scallions, sliced into strips

red bell pepper strips

Serves 4
Preparation time: 30 minutes
Cooking time: 8–10 minutes

globe artichokes with garlic & herb mayonnaise

1 First make the garlic and herb mayonnaise. Put the mayonnaise into a bowl, stir in the garlic and mixed herbs, and leave to stand for at least 30 minutes.

2 Discard the large base stalks from the artichokes and rub the cut surface with lemon to prevent discoloring. Put the artichokes in a large pot of boiling water. Squeeze the juice from the lemon quarters into the pot and drop the lemon pieces in, too. Cook the artichokes for 25–30 minutes, or until a leaf can be pulled out easily. Using a slotted spoon, remove the artichokes and leave them upside down to drain and cool slightly.

3 Cut each artichoke into 4 wedges. Discard the hairy choke. Arrange the artichoke quarters on individual plates or on a large platter. Drizzle the olive oil over them, and add salt and pepper. Serve with garlic and herb mayonnaise for dipping. Garnish with lemon wedges.

4 globe artichokes

1 lemon, quartered

¼ cup olive oil

salt and pepper

Garlic & Herb Mayonnaise:

1¼ cups ready-made mayonnaise (or see page 9)

2 garlic cloves, crushed

2 tablespoons finely chopped mixed tarragon, chives, and parsley

lemon wedges, to garnish

Serves 4

Preparation time: 15 minutes plus standing

Cooking time: 25–30 minutes

classic paella ●

mussels in white wine sauce ●

pan-fried salmon with tomato coulis ●

lobster & asparagus salad ●

monkfish & vegetable parcels with saffron sauce ●

lobster thermidor ●

trout with almonds ●

skate in orange & cider sauce ●

seafood risotto ●

sole bonne femme ●

normandy-style sole ●

salmon with three sauces ●

thai steamed fish curry ●

fish & shellfish

classic paella

1 Put the garlic slices in a large pan with the herbs, wine, ⅔ cup of the stock, and season with salt and pepper. Add the mussels, cover the pan tightly, and bring to a boil. Shake the pan and simmer for 5 minutes, or until the mussels open. Remove the mussels and set aside, discarding any that remain closed. Strain the liquid and set aside.

2 Heat half of the oil in a pan and fry the squid for 5 minutes, stirring frequently. Add the onion, red pepper, and crushed garlic, and cook gently, stirring frequently, for 5 minutes. Add the mussel liquid and tomatoes, and season. Bring to a boil, then simmer, stirring, for 15–20 minutes until thick. Transfer to a bowl.

3 Heat the remaining oil in a large sauté pan or frying pan, and fry the chicken for 5 minutes. Add the rice, and turn it in the oil for 3 minutes. Stir in the squid mixture. Add about one-third of the remaining stock, and bring to a boil, stirring constantly. Boil rapidly for about 3–4 minutes, then cover the pan and simmer for 30 minutes. Add more stock as the rice becomes dry, and stir frequently. The paella is ready when the chicken is cooked, the rice is tender but still firm, and almost all the liquid has been absorbed.

4 Add the peas and shrimp, if using, and simmer, stirring, for 5 minutes or until cooked, adding more stock, if required. Arrange the mussels on top of the paella, cover the pan tightly with foil, and cook for 5 minutes, or until the mussels are hot. Serve garnished with the chopped parsley and the parsley sprigs.

4 garlic cloves (2 sliced, 2 crushed)

1 bunch of fresh mixed herbs

⅔ cup dry white wine

just over 2 quarts hot chicken stock

2 lb. fresh mussels, cleaned (see page 32)

¼ cup extra-virgin olive oil

4 small squid, cleaned, and sliced into rings

1 large onion, finely chopped

1 red bell pepper, cored, seeded, and chopped

4 large ripe tomatoes, peeled, seeded, and chopped

12 skinned and boned chicken thighs, cut into bite-size pieces

1 lb. (2⅔ cups) Arborio rice

1 cup fresh or frozen peas

12 large raw shrimp, peeled (optional)

salt and pepper

To Garnish:

1 tablespoon chopped flat-leaf parsley

parsley sprigs

Serves 6
Preparation time: about 40 minutes
Cooking time: about 1¼ hours

mussels in white wine sauce

1 Scrub the mussels with a stiff brush, and scrape off the beards and barnacles with a small, sharp knife. Discard any open mussels.

2 Melt half the butter in a large heavy pot and gently fry the onion, garlic, and leek, until soft but not colored. Add the mussels, wine, and water, cover, and bring to a boil. Cook for 2–5 minutes, or until the mussels open, shaking the pan several times during the cooking. Divide the mussels among 4 large soup bowls, discarding any that have not opened during cooking. Keep hot.

3 Mix the remaining butter with the flour to form a paste and, little by little, add to the juices in the pot, stirring to thicken.

4 Bring the mussel liquid to a boil, season with salt and pepper to taste, stir in the parsley, and pour this over the mussels. For extra richness, 1–2 tablespoons heavy cream can be added to the sauce just before serving, if you like.

4 lb. mussels

½ stick (¼ cup) butter

1 large onion, finely chopped

1–2 garlic cloves, finely chopped

1 small leek, white and green parts, finely sliced

1¼ cups dry white wine

⅔ cup water

¼ cup all-purpose flour

2 tablespoons finely chopped flat-leaf parsley

1–2 tablespoons heavy cream (optional)

salt and pepper

Serves 4
Preparation time: 20 minutes
Cooking time: 10 minutes

1 To make the tomato coulis, place all the ingredients, except the lemon juice, in a pot and bring to a boil. Reduce the heat, cover, and simmer for about 10 minutes until very soft. Remove the bouquet garni.

2 Purée the coulis in a food processor, then press it through a strainer. Return to a boil, and reduce to a sauce-like consistency. Add the lemon juice, and season to taste.

3 Heat the oil in a frying pan and sauté the garlic for a few minutes to flavor the oil, then discard the garlic. Season the salmon with salt, pepper, and nutmeg, add to the pan, and sauté over a high heat for a few seconds on each side. Reduce the heat and cook for a few minutes, until the fish is cooked through. Remove and keep warm. Pour the wine, if using, into the pan, stir to mix with the juices, then pour the contents into the coulis.

4 Serve the salmon with salad leaves and dill sprigs, and spoon the tomato coulis beside it.

1 tablespoon olive oil

1 garlic clove, crushed

2 salmon steaks

grated nutmeg, to taste

⅓ cup red wine (optional)

salt and pepper

Tomato Coulis:

1½ lb. (2¼ cups) sliced ripe tomatoes

1 small onion, finely chopped

pinch of sugar

1 bouquet garni

juice of ½ lemon

salt and pepper

To Serve:

mixed salad leaves

dill sprigs

Serves 2
Preparation time: 20 minutes
Cooking time: 10–15 minutes

pan-fried salmon with tomato coulis

lobster & asparagus salad

1 First make the dressing. Put the garlic, anchovies, and herbs into a food processor, and blend well. Add the mayonnaise, and blend to mix. Add the vinegar, and salt and pepper to taste. Transfer to a bowl, cover, and chill for at least 1 hour. Before serving, stir in a few tablespoons of sour cream, if you like.

2 Trim the ends from the asparagus spears, making them all the same length. Then, if necessary, scrape the sides of each spear with a swivel-bladed potato peeler, starting about 2 inches from the tip. Cook the asparagus in a pan of salted, boiling water for 4–8 minutes, depending on size, or until tender but still crisp. Drain and rinse under cold running water, then drain again. Leave to cool.

3 Crack the claws and tails of the lobsters, and remove the meat. Keep the claw meat whole, and slice the tail meat across into neat rounds.

4 Arrange the asparagus spears and lobster meat on a bed of salad leaves. Spoon a little of the dressing over them, and serve the rest separately.

1 lb. asparagus spears (16–20 spears)

2 lobsters, 1–1½ lb. each, freshly cooked

mixed salad leaves, to serve

Herb Dressing:

1 small garlic clove, crushed

2 anchovies, well drained

1 tablespoon snipped chives

1 tablespoon chopped parsley

1 teaspoon chopped tarragon

½ cup mayonnaise

1 teaspoon tarragon vinegar

a few tablespoons sour cream (optional)

salt and pepper

Serves 2

Preparation time: 20 minutes plus chilling

Cooking time: 5 minutes

monkfish & vegetable parcels with saffron sauce

1 To make the saffron sauce, put the wine in a small saucepan, add the shallot, and boil until the wine is reduced to about ½ tablespoon. Remove from the heat, stir in the cream and saffron, and set aside.

2 Cut out four large pieces of foil and lightly butter them. Cut the monkfish into medallions. Arrange a few medallions in the center of each piece of foil and surround them with small bundles of the prepared vegetables. Sprinkle with the lemon juice and wine, and season lightly with salt and pepper. Bring the corners of the foil together and crimp the edges, so that the parcels are totally sealed.

3 Place the parcels in a steamer over a pan of boiling water, and steam for about 10 minutes, or until the fish is tender.

4 Open the parcels and pour a quarter of the saffron sauce over each portion of fish—the juices and sauce mingle and taste delicious. Serve hot, garnished with parsley sprigs.

1 lb. monkfish, skinned and boned

2 carrots, cut into matchsticks

2 celery stalks, cut into matchsticks

1 onion, very finely sliced into half rings

1 red bell pepper, cored, seeded, and cut into matchsticks

2 tablespoons lemon juice

3 tablespoons white wine

salt and pepper

flat-leaf parsley sprigs, to garnish

Saffron Sauce:

⅓ cup dry white wine

1 shallot, finely chopped

⅓ cup heavy cream

pinch of powdered saffron

Serves 4
Preparation time: 20 minutes
Cooking time: about 20 minutes

lobster thermidor

1 Cut the lobster lengthwise in half and remove the meat from the shell. Cut it up into pieces about ½ inch long (you will find this easier if you cut the meat at an angle). Wash and dry the shells. Heat half of the butter in a small frying pan and add the lobster. Fry gently, turning occasionally.

2 Meanwhile, heat the remaining butter in a small pan, add the onion, and fry gently until soft. Add the flour, and blend thoroughly. Add the milk to the pan, stirring, and bring to a boil. Simmer for a few minutes, then add the Cheddar. Mix thoroughly over a low heat, then add the wine and paprika. Season with salt and pepper.

3 Pour the sauce over the lobster in the frying pan, and mix well. Cook over a low heat for a few minutes. Place the cleaned lobster shells on a broiler rack, then spoon the lobster mixture into them. Sprinkle thickly with Parmesan, and place under a preheated broiler. Cook until the sauce is bubbling and golden brown. Arrange a bed of salad leaves on 2 serving plates, place the lobster on top, and garnish with lemon wedges.

2 lb. lobster, cooked

½ stick (¼ cup) butter

1 small onion, finely chopped

¼ cup all-purpose flour

⅔ cup milk

¼ cup grated Cheddar cheese

1 tablespoon white wine

pinch of paprika

2 tablespoons grated Parmesan cheese

salt and pepper

To Garnish:

salad leaves

lemon wedges

Serves 2
Preparation time: 45 minutes
Cooking time: 20 minutes

■ It is not easy to cut a lobster neatly in half, so ask your fish seller to do it for you.

trout with almonds

1 Season the flour with salt and pepper, and dust it over the trout.

2 Heat half of the butter in a large pan and fry the trout for about 3–4 minutes on each side. Remove the trout from the pan and keep warm.

3 Add the rest of the butter to the frying pan, along with the flaked almonds, and fry gently until the almonds have turned golden. Add the lemon juice, and season to taste with salt and pepper, then heat the sauce thoroughly and pour it over the trout. Garnish with fennel sprigs and lemon wedges, and serve at once.

all-purpose flour, for coating

4 medium trout, cleaned

1 stick (½ cup) butter

¾ to 1 cup flaked almonds

2 tablespoons lemon juice

salt and pepper

To Garnish:

fennel sprigs

lemon wedges

Serves 4
Preparation time: 15 minutes
Cooking time: about 20 minutes

skate in orange & cider sauce

1 Place the skate wings in a large shallow pan. Add the onion, cider, orange juice and zest, then a pinch of salt and pepper. Bring slowly up to a barely simmering point, and poach for about 15 minutes.

2 Lift out the skate wings with a slotted spoon, place them on a warmed serving dish, and keep warm.

3 Turn up the heat, add the capers, and boil the cooking liquor until it is reduced and thick, then taste and adjust the seasoning, if necessary. Add a squeeze of lemon juice, remove from the heat, and swirl in the cream. Pour the sauce over the skate and serve immediately, garnished with the orange segments. Serve with green vegetables, if you like.

4 skate wings

1 small onion, finely chopped

1¼ cups dry cider

juice and finely pared zest of 1 orange

salt and pepper

1 tablespoon capers

a squeeze of lemon juice

¼ cup heavy cream

orange segments, peeled and quartered, to garnish

Serves 4
Preparation time: 15 minutes
Cooking time: 20 minutes

■ The delicate shape and texture of the skate wing make it perfect to serve for a special meal. Skate is best poached, steamed, or shallow-fried.

1 To prepare the seafood, wash and clean the octopus or squid, and slice them into rings. Cut the tentacles into small pieces. Wash, peel, and devein the shrimp. Cut the fish into large chunks.

2 Heat the oil in a large pan and fry the onion and garlic gently, until soft and golden. Add the rice, and stir for 1–2 minutes.

3 Add some of the stock and the chopped tomatoes, and bring to a boil. Reduce the heat and simmer gently, stirring in more stock, as and when necessary, until all the liquid has been absorbed and the rice is tender. After 15 minutes, add the prepared seafood. Stir in the parsley, and season with salt and pepper when the rice is cooked.

4 Cut the chiles into thin strips and use as a garnish. Serve the risotto with lime wedges.

2 lb. mixed seafood (octopus, squid, shrimp, white fish)

2 tablespoons olive oil

1 large onion, chopped

2 garlic cloves, crushed

1⅓ cups Arborio rice

2½–4 cups fish stock

3 tomatoes, peeled and chopped

2 tablespoons finely chopped flat-leaf parsley

salt and pepper

To Serve:

4 red or green chiles

lime wedges

Serves 4
Preparation time: 15 minutes
Cooking time: 45 minutes

seafood risotto

sole bonne femme

1 Melt two-thirds of the butter in a pan, and shallow-fry the shallots and mushrooms. Stir in the parsley, then spread the mixture evenly over the base of an ovenproof, flameproof dish or cast-iron pan.

2 Roll up the sole fillets from head to tail, put them into the dish, and season well with salt and pepper. Pour over them the white wine, stock, and lemon juice, and bake in a preheated oven, 350°F, for 15 minutes.

3 Transfer the sole to a warmed serving dish and place the dish in which it was cooked over medium heat on the stove. Mix the remaining butter with the flour to form a paste. Add it in small knobs to the boiling mushroom mixture, and whisk until the butter melts and the sauce thickens.

4 Pour the sauce over the sole and serve hot, garnished with parsley sprigs and lemon twists, and a selection of seasonal green vegetables.

¾ stick (⅓ cup) butter

4 shallots, chopped

a generous cup sliced mushrooms

2 tablespoons chopped parsley

2 lb. sole fillets, cut in half lengthwise and skinned

¼ cup dry white wine

⅔ cup fish stock

2 tablespoons lemon juice

¼ cup all-purpose flour

salt and pepper

To Garnish:

parsley sprigs

lemon twists

Serves 4–6
Preparation time: 20 minutes
Cooking time: about 30 minutes

normandy-
style sole

1 Season the fillets with salt and pepper. Melt ¼ stick of the butter in a flameproof casserole, add the fillets and mushrooms, sprinkle with the lemon juice, and pour in the hot stock. Cover, and bake in a preheated oven, 350°F, for 12–15 minutes, or until the sole is tender. Remove the fish and mushrooms, and keep warm. Set aside the stock.

2 Put the mussels into a large pot with the shallots and wine. Cook over a high heat until the shells open, shaking the pot. Discard any that do not open. Remove half of the mussels from their shells. Keep all the mussels warm. Strain the cooking juices from the mussels and the sole into a pan, and boil steadily until reduced by three-quarters. Remove from the heat.

3 Mix together the egg yolks and cream, and stir them into the cooking juices. Cook over a low heat, stirring, for 3–4 minutes; do not boil. Remove from the heat and whisk in the remaining butter, a little at a time.

4 Arrange the sole fillets, shelled mussels, and shrimp on four warmed plates. Pour the sauce over them, and garnish with the mussels in their shells, chopped parsley, parsley sprigs, and lemon slices.

four 10-oz. Dover soles, filleted

1¼ sticks (⅔ cup) butter

a generous cup mushrooms

1 tablespoon lemon juice

2½ cups hot fish stock

2 lb. mussels, cleaned (see page 32)

4 shallots, finely chopped

⅔ cup dry white wine

2 egg yolks

a scant cup heavy cream

a scant cup cooked peeled shrimp

salt and pepper

To Garnish:

2 tablespoons chopped parsley

parsley sprigs

lemon slices

Serves 4

Preparation time: 15 minutes

Cooking time: 1 hour

salmon with three sauces

1 Wash the salmon belly cavity, then pat dry with paper towels, and season lightly with salt and pepper. Grease a sheet of foil with the butter. Put the salmon on the foil, wrap it up, and place in a baking dish. Bake in a preheated oven, 300°F, for about 1 hour. Remove from the oven and leave to cool.

2 Meanwhile, prepare the sauces. To make the avocado sauce, place the avocado, yogurt, salt and pepper, and lemon juice to taste, in a food processor and blend until smooth. To make the other sauces, mix the ingredients together, season, and chill until ready to serve.

3 Remove the salmon carefully from the foil and put it on a large cutting board. Using a thin-bladed, sharp knife, cut through the skin along the backbone, across the tail, and around the head. Using the knife blade, remove the skin and the fins. With the back of the knife, scrape away the brown-colored flesh in the center. Turn the salmon over and repeat. Then cut down along the backbone of the fish, turn the knife flat, and ease the fillet gently from the bone, and lift off. (This may have to be done in two pieces.) At the head and tail, cut through the bone with kitchen scissors, and peel away. Replace the upper fillet. Slice the salmon into portions.

4 Place a slice of salmon on each plate and pour pools of the sauces next to it. Garnish with cucumber and lemon slices, and dill and chervil sprigs.

1 salmon, about 4 lb., cleaned

½ stick (¼ cup) butter, melted

lettuce leaves, to serve

salt and pepper

Avocado Sauce:

1 ripe avocado, peeled and pitted

⅔ cup plain yogurt

2–4 tablespoons lemon juice

Horseradish Sauce:

1–2 tablespoons grated horseradish

⅔ cup sour cream

½ cup chopped walnuts

Cocktail Sauce:

1–2 tablespoons tomato ketchup

⅔ cup mayonnaise

a few drops of Tabasco sauce

To Garnish:

thin cucumber slices (see page 8)

thin lemon slices (see page 8)

dill sprigs

chervil sprigs

Serves 8–10

Preparation time: about 1 hour plus chilling

Cooking time: about 1 hour

thai steamed fish curry

1 Mix together the Thai red curry paste, coconut milk, fish sauce, and beaten egg. Set aside.

2 Place the fish pieces in a shallow, non-metallic dish. Add the cilantro, mint, and Thai sweet basil, and gently mix together. Pour the curry paste mixture over the fish, and stir to coat evenly.

3 Scatter the lime zest and chile slices over the fish. Cover the dish with foil, and steam over boiling water for 15 minutes, or until the fish is just cooked through. The egg will lightly thicken the sauce. Serve immediately with rice.

3 tablespoons Thai red curry paste

a scant cup coconut milk

1 tablespoon fish sauce (nam pla)

1 egg, beaten

1 lb. skinless cod or halibut fillets, cut into 2-inch pieces

1 tablespoon chopped cilantro

1 tablespoon chopped mint

1 tablespoon chopped Thai sweet basil

1 tablespoon grated lime zest

1 large green chile, seeded and finely sliced

1 large red chile, seeded and finely sliced

plain boiled rice, to serve

Serves 4
Preparation time: 10 minutes
Cooking time: 15 minutes

■ Banana leaves add a touch of the exotic when serving Thai meals. Whole leaves can be purchased from Thai or Asian stores. Dip in boiling water to soften before serving.

vegetables in malaysian coconut sauce •

spinach & mushroom roulade •

mediterranean vegetable salad •

spicy eggplants with tomatoes •

leek terrine with walnuts & feta •

seasonal vegetable medley •

wild mushrooms in crispy cases •

vegetable terrine •

camembert & cranberry pie •

tagliatelle with mushrooms & cream •

wild mushroom salad with croûtons •

vegetarian

1 First make the coconut sauce. Put the tamarind into a bowl. Pour the boiling water over it, and leave to soak for 30 minutes. Mash the tamarind in the soaking water, then strain through a mesh strainer that's been set over a bowl, and press the tamarind to extract as much pulp as possible.

2 Skim 2 tablespoons of the cream from the coconut milk, and place it in a wok or heavy-based pan. Add the curry paste, ginger, onion, and turmeric, and cook over gentle heat, stirring, for 2–3 minutes. Stir in the remaining coconut milk and the tamarind liquid. Bring to a boil, then lower the heat and season with salt.

3 Add the broccoli to the sauce and cook for 5 minutes, then add the green beans and red pepper, and cook, stirring, for a further 5 minutes. Finally, stir in the zucchini and cook for 1–2 minutes. Shrimp chips (krupuk) make a nice accompaniment.

2 heaped cups broccoli florets

¾ cup green beans, cut into 1-inch lengths

1 red bell pepper, cored, seeded, and sliced

¾ cup thinly sliced zucchini

Coconut Sauce:

2 tablespoons tamarind pulp

⅔ cup boiling water

a 14-oz. can thick coconut milk

2 teaspoons Thai green curry paste

1 teaspoon grated ginger

1 onion, diced

½ teaspoon ground turmeric

salt

Serves 4
Preparation time: 15 minutes plus soaking
Cooking time: about 20 minutes

vegetables in malaysian coconut sauce

■ Tamarind pulp is available at large supermarkets and Asian and Indian food stores. Its sweet and sour flavor adds a delicious bite to many dishes. Use lemon juice or vinegar as a substitute.

spinach & mushroom roulade

1 Line a 12 x 8-inch baking sheet with sides with wax paper, or make a lining of the same measurements with aluminum foil. Put the spinach into a pot with the knob of butter, and cook until soft. Drain the spinach well, chop, and transfer to a large bowl. Add the egg yolks, beating them well into the chopped spinach, and season to taste with salt and pepper.

2 Whisk the egg whites in a large grease-free bowl until just holding their shape. Using a metal spoon, quickly fold them into the spinach mixture. Spoon the mixture into the prepared baking sheet, sprinkle with the grated Parmesan, and bake in a preheated oven, 400°F, for 10 minutes.

3 Meanwhile, make the filling. Heat the butter in a small pan. Add the sliced mushrooms and cook gently until softened. Stir in the flour and cook, stirring constantly, for 1 minute. Slowly stir in the milk, and cook the sauce until thickened. Stir in the nutmeg and season to taste.

4 Remove the spinach roulade from the oven and invert it onto a sheet of wax paper. Quickly spread the mushroom filling over the surface, then gently roll up the roulade. Cut into thick slices, and serve immediately with a salad garnish.

1 lb. fresh spinach

1 tablespoon butter

4 eggs, separated

½ cup grated Parmesan cheese

salt and pepper

salad leaves, to garnish

Filling:

1 tablespoon butter

1¾ cups sliced mushrooms

1 tablespoon all-purpose flour

⅔ cup milk

pinch of grated nutmeg

Serves 4
Preparation time: 15 minutes
Cooking time: about 20 minutes

mediterranean vegetable salad

1   Put the fennel and onions into a large pot of boiling water. When the water returns to a boil, cook the vegetables for 1 minute. Add the zucchini strips and cook for 1 minute more. Drain in a colander and rinse under cold running water, then drain again, and set aside.

2   Combine the olive oil, lemon zest, and thyme in a large bowl. Add all the vegetables, and toss lightly to coat them in the flavored oil.

3   Line a broiler pan with foil. Spread the vegetable mixture evenly in a single layer in the pan, and cook under a preheated hot broiler for about 15 minutes, turning frequently, until the vegetables are tender and patched with brown. Leave to cool.

4   To make the dressing, whisk all the ingredients together in a small bowl. Arrange the cooled vegetables on individual plates or on a serving platter. Pour the dressing over the vegetables, and serve.

2 small fennel bulbs, cut into wedges

2 red onions, cut into wedges

3 zucchini, cut in half, and sliced lengthwise into strips

¼ cup extra-virgin olive oil

1 teaspoon finely grated lemon zest

1 tablespoon chopped thyme

1 red or yellow bell pepper, cored, seeded, and cut into wide strips

a generous cup of cherry tomatoes, cut in half

Dressing:

¼ cup extra-virgin olive oil

2 tablespoons lemon juice

pinch of sugar

1 tablespoon chopped oregano

salt and pepper

Serves 4

Preparation time: 15 minutes

Cooking time: about 25 minutes

1½ lb. eggplants, cut into 1½-inch chunks

¼ cup lemon juice

¾ cup butter or ghee

2 onions, thinly sliced

4 garlic cloves, thinly sliced

3-inch piece fresh ginger, peeled and thinly sliced

2 teaspoons black onion seeds

3-inch piece cinnamon stick

2 teaspoons coriander seeds

2 teaspoons cumin seeds

2 teaspoons ground pepper

2 teaspoons salt

2 teaspoons garam masala

1½ teaspoons ground turmeric

1 teaspoon ground red pepper

a 13-oz. can chopped tomatoes

½ cup tomato paste

2½ cups boiling water

dried red chiles, to garnish

Serves 4–6

Preparation time: 15 minutes

Cooking time: 25–30 minutes

1 Place the eggplants in a bowl and stir in the lemon juice.

2 Melt the butter or ghee in a large wok, add the onions, garlic, and ginger, and fry gently for 4–5 minutes until just soft. Add the black onion seeds, cinnamon, coriander, and cumin seeds, and stir thoroughly. Fry for a further 2 minutes, then stir in the pepper, salt, garam masala, turmeric, and ground red pepper.

3 Add the tomatoes with their juices and the tomato paste, stir well, and bring to a boil. Pour in the boiling water and stir in the eggplant pieces with the lemon juice. Bring to a boil, lower the heat, and simmer gently for 15–20 minutes, or until soft. Garnish with the dried red chiles, and serve hot.

spicy eggplants with tomatoes

leek terrine with walnuts & feta

1 Cut off the roots and most of the green part of the leeks. Split the leeks horizontally to within 2 inches of the root end. Rinse the leaves under running cold water to wash out any grit or mud. Boil the leeks in salted water for 10 minutes, or until tender.

2 Fill a 1-lb. loaf pan with the leeks laid alternately head to tail, sprinkling each layer with salt and pepper. Put a second pan inside the first, pressing down the leeks. Invert both pans so that the water can drain out. Chill for at least 4 hours with a 2-lb. weight on top.

3 Carefully turn out the leek terrine. Using a very sharp knife, cut it into six thick slices. Lay each slice on a plate and surround them with the salad leaves. Scatter the walnuts and crumbled feta cheese on top of the salad leaves.

4 To make the dressing, combine all the ingredients in a small bowl, season with salt and pepper, then spoon it over the salad. Garnish with the parsley sprigs and chives.

20 small young leeks

radicchio or other salad leaves

½ cup chopped walnuts

¾ cup crumbled feta cheese

salt and pepper

Dressing:

¼ cup olive oil

2 tablespoons walnut oil

2 tablespoons wine vinegar

2 tablespoons English mustard

To Garnish:

flat-leaf parsley sprigs

chives

Serves 6

Preparation time: 25 minutes plus chilling

Cooking time: 10 minutes

½ stick (¼ cup) butter

1 tablespoon chopped herbs, such as mint and parsley

4 zucchini, cut in half lengthwise

2 leeks, trimmed, washed, and sliced

2 large carrots, cut into thick matchsticks

¾ cup green beans, topped and tailed

4 celery stalks, cut into thick matchsticks

1 small bunch watercress, trimmed

salt and pepper

1 Mix the butter with the herbs, and season well with salt and pepper. Place the zucchini, leeks, carrots, beans, and celery in a steamer, then season well with salt and pepper.

2 Cover, and steam over boiling water for 3–5 minutes. Add the watercress, and steam for 1 minute more. Transfer to a warmed serving dish and dot with the herb butter.

Serves 4

Preparation time: 20 minutes

Cooking time: 5 minutes

seasonal vegetable medley

wild mushrooms in crispy cases

1 Brush both sides of the bread with the butter. Press into 8 tartlet molds and bake in a preheated oven, 400°F, for 10–15 minutes, until crisp and golden brown.

2 Meanwhile, make the filing. Melt the butter in a small saucepan, add the shallot, and fry for about 5 minutes until softened. Add the mushrooms, and cook for a further 5 minutes, until tender. Stir in the Madeira and allow to bubble briefly, then stir in the cream and chopped parsley, along with salt and pepper to taste. Cook over a moderate heat for a few minutes, until the mixture forms a sauce.

3 Arrange the salad leaves on small plates and place a bread case on each one. Fill with the mushroom mixture, and serve warm.

Crispy Cases:

8 thin slices of bread, crusts removed

½ stick (¼ cup) butter, melted

Filling:

2 tablespoons butter

1 shallot, chopped

1¾ cups sliced mushrooms (chestnut, oyster, shiitake)

1 tablespoon Madeira

¼ cup heavy cream

1 tablespoon chopped parsley

salt and pepper

assorted salad leaves, to serve

Serves 6–8
Preparation time: 15 minutes
Cooking time: 10–15 minutes

1 Grease a small bread pan with butter, and line with wax paper, large enough to extend up the sides. Cook the carrots and beans in separate saucepans in 1½ inches of boiling water, until tender. Cook the spinach in a dry saucepan for 3–4 minutes.

2 Drain the vegetables thoroughly, reserving the water, then purée each separately, adding 1 egg yolk to each mixture. Add the cream to the puréed fava beans. Season with salt and pepper, and add a little nutmeg to the spinach purée. Spoon the spinach into the prepared pan, leveling to make a smooth layer. Carefully spoon the fava bean purée in an even layer on top, and finally add the carrot purée. Cover with foil and bake in a preheated oven, 325°F, for 1 hour, removing the foil after about 45 minutes. The pâté should be firm in the center when touched lightly; leave to cool in the pan.

3 To make the sauce, put the pepper under a hot broiler until the skin is blackened and blistered all over. Then place in cold water and peel off the skin. Remove the stalk and rinse away the seeds. Purée in a blender with a scant cup of the reserved cooking water. Season to taste, and chill until ready to serve.

4 Slip a knife around the sides of the pâté to loosen it, then tip it out of the pan, and strip off the wax paper. Cut into slices, and place one on each plate on top of a pool of sauce. Garnish with the dill sprigs and the lime twists.

vegetable terrine

butter, for greasing

1½ cups carrots, cut into even-size pieces

½ lb. fava beans, shelled (to yield around ½ cup)

10 oz. frozen spinach, defrosted

3 egg yolks

3 tablespoons heavy cream

freshly grated nutmeg

salt and pepper

Sauce:

1 large red pepper

To Garnish:

dill sprigs

lime twists

Serves 6

Preparation time: 40 minutes

Cooking time: 1½ hours

camembert & cranberry pie

1 Place the cranberries in a small saucepan with the sugar, water, and port. Bring to a boil, then lower the heat and simmer gently until the cranberries pop and are just tender. This should take about 5 minutes. Leave to cool.

2 Layer the phyllo dough on a greased baking sheet, brushing each layer with melted butter and arranging each sheet at a slightly different angle from the previous one, to form points all around the edge. Place the Camembert in the center and spread the cranberry sauce over the top. Season with pepper.

3 Gather up the phyllo dough over the cheese and cranberry mixture, scrunching the edges together. Brush with the remaining butter, and bake in a preheated oven, 400°F, for 15–20 minutes, or until golden. Cool the pie on the baking sheet for 5 minutes, then cut into wedges to serve.

■ Fresh cranberries will keep well in the refrigerator for up to 4 weeks in an unopened bag, or for about 1 week once opened, but remove damaged fruit first.

¾ cup cranberries

2 tablespoons sugar

3 tablespoons water

1 tablespoon port

8 sheets phyllo dough

2 tablespoons butter, melted

1 whole Camembert cheese, about ½ lb.

pepper

Serves 4
Preparation time: 20 minutes
Cooking time: 15–20 minutes

tagliatelle with mushrooms & cream

1 Put the porcini in a bowl, cover with the warm water, and let soak for 20–30 minutes. Drain, reserving the liquid, then chop into small pieces.

2 Heat the butter in a large pan and fry the garlic and onion until soft, then add the porcini and fry gently for a few minutes. Stir in 3 tablespoons of the reserved liquid and add the cremini mushrooms. Cover the pan, turn up the heat so the mushrooms produce their own juices, and cook, stirring occasionally, until the mushrooms are soft, then add the cream, season with salt and pepper, and heat through.

3 Meanwhile, bring a large pot of lightly salted water to a boil, add the tagliatelle, and cook for about 10–12 minutes, or according to package instructions, until just tender.

4 Drain and transfer the pasta to a warmed serving dish. Reheat the sauce, pour it over the pasta, and garnish with chives.

■ If dried cèpe mushrooms (porcini) are not available, use fresh cèpes, which will last for up to 1 week, if refrigerated.

½ oz. dried porcini mushrooms

2 cups warm water

3 tablespoons butter

1 garlic clove, crushed

¼ cup finely chopped onion

3½ cups finely sliced cremini mushrooms

⅔ cup heavy cream

10–12 oz. tagliatelle

butter, to taste

salt and pepper

1 tablespoon chopped chives, to garnish

Serves 3

Preparation time: 10 minutes plus soaking

Cooking time: 15–20 minutes

wild mushroom salad with croûtons

1   To prepare the mushrooms, leave small ones whole but slice or chop the larger ones.

2   To make the croûtons, cut the bread into small cubes. Heat the oil with the butter in a frying pan until sizzling. Add the bread cubes and fry, stirring constantly, for 3–4 minutes, or until crisp and golden. Drain on paper towels, and sprinkle with salt to taste.

3   Heat the olive oil in a large frying pan. Add the shallot and cook over a moderate heat for 3–4 minutes, until softened. Stir in the garlic and cook for a further 1 minute. Add the mushrooms and thyme, season with salt and pepper, and cook, stirring, for 2 minutes. Add the water and cook over a moderate heat, stirring frequently, for about 5 minutes, or until the mushrooms are tender. Transfer to a bowl and leave to cool.

4   When the mushroom mixture has cooled, add the arugula or watercress, basil, and croûtons to the bowl. Toss lightly to mix. Drizzle the dressing over the salad and serve sprinkled with chopped parsley, if you like.

1 lb. mixed wild mushrooms or cultivated mushrooms

¼ cup olive oil

1 shallot, finely chopped

1 garlic clove, chopped

1 teaspoon chopped thyme

¼ cup water

a large handful of arugula or watercress

handful of basil leaves, roughly torn

6 tablespoons French vinaigrette dressing

chopped parsley, to garnish (optional)

salt and pepper

Croûtons:

3 thick slices white bread, crusts removed

2 tablespoons light olive oil

2 tablespoons butter

Serves 4

Preparation time: 15 minutes

Cooking time: about 12 minutes

guinea fowl with fresh gnocchi ●

duck with orange ●

braised pheasant with marsala & chestnuts ●

chicken with artichokes ●

tandoori chicken ●

chicken vindaloo ●

spicy duck in port with fresh figs ●

roast pheasant flambéed with calvados ●

chicken in red wine ●

burgundy-style beef ●

beef & new potato salad ●

lamb & apricot tagine ●

noisettes of lamb with pomegranate ●

tournedos en croûte ●

tenderloin steak with smoked oysters ●

roghan ghosht ●

poultry & meat

1 Roll the guinea fowl in the flour, shaking off any excess. Heat the oil in a large flameproof casserole, over a moderate heat, add the guinea fowl, in batches, and brown well. Remove with a slotted spoon and set aside. Lower the heat, add the shallots, garlic, and sage, and cook gently for 5 minutes until soft. Add the wine and bring to a boil, stirring. Return the guinea fowl to the casserole, along with the stock and bay leaf. Bring back to a boil, reduce the heat, cover, and simmer for 25–30 minutes.

2 To make the gnocchi, place the potatoes in a pot of water, bring to a boil, and cook for 20–25 minutes. Drain well and peel. While still warm, purée them in a food processor or press them through a strainer or food mill into a bowl. Beat the egg and parsley into the mixture. Add the flour slowly (you may not need all of it) until smooth and slightly sticky. Season with salt. Roll the mixture into a long sausage about ½ inch in diameter. Cut into ¾-inch lengths. Take one piece at a time, and press it onto a floured fork. Roll along the prongs and off the fork onto a floured tray. Set aside.

3 To cook the mushrooms, gently melt the butter in a pan, add the shallot, and cook until soft. Add the mushrooms, lemon zest and juice, and cook until soft. Stir into the casserole 10 minutes before the end of cooking.

4 Bring a large pot of water to a boil and drop in 20–25 pieces of gnocchi at a time. They will quickly rise. Cook for 10–15 seconds. When ready, drain and keep warm while cooking the rest. Serve with the hot casserole.

1 plump guinea fowl, cut into 8 pieces

2 tablespoons seasoned flour

2 tablespoons olive oil

2 shallots, finely chopped

1 garlic clove, crushed

2 tablespoons chopped sage

1 cup dry white wine

1 cup chicken stock

1 bay leaf

salt and pepper

Gnocchi:

1½ lb. large potatoes, unpeeled

1 egg, beaten

3 tablespoons chopped parsley

1 cup all-purpose flour, sifted

Mushrooms:

½ stick (¼ cup) butter

1 shallot, finely chopped

1 lb. mixed mushrooms, cut into halves or quarters if large (around 5–6 cups)

finely grated zest of 1 lemon

2 tablespoons lemon juice

Serves 4	
Preparation time: 1 hour	
Cooking time: 1 hour	

guinea fowl with fresh gnocchi

2 tablespoons butter

3 tablespoons olive oil

a 4-lb. duck, trussed with string

4 garlic cloves, crushed

¼ lb. Canadian bacon, cut into thin strips

2½ cups dry white wine

a scant cup chicken stock

1 bouquet garni

zest and juice of 2 oranges

1 tablespoon wine vinegar

1 tablespoon flour

2 tablespoons butter, softened

salt and pepper

To Garnish:

2 oranges, thinly sliced

watercress sprigs

Serves 6
Preparation time: 10 minutes
Cooking time: 1¾ hours

duck with orange

1 Heat the butter and oil in a deep flameproof casserole or cast-iron pan, and add the duck. Fry over medium heat, turning the duck when necessary, until it is golden brown all over.

2 Add the garlic and Canadian bacon to the casserole, and fry for about 1–2 minutes. Add the white wine and stock, bring to a boil, then simmer for 3–4 minutes, or until slightly reduced. Add the bouquet garni and orange juice, season with salt and pepper, then cover the casserole. Reduce the heat and simmer gently, basting occasionally, for 1½ hours, or until the duck is cooked.

3 Meanwhile, using a sharp knife, cut the orange zest into fine strips and blanch for 5 minutes in a small pan of boiling water. Remove and drain, then dry thoroughly on paper towels and set aside.

4 Blend the flour and butter in a bowl. Remove the duck from the casserole, cut it into serving pieces, and keep warm. Boil the cooking liquid for about 10 minutes, until reduced. Add the vinegar, orange zest, and little pieces of the flour and butter mixture, stirring constantly, until the sauce thickens. Serve the duck with the sauce, garnished with orange slices and watercress sprigs.

braised pheasant with marsala & chestnuts

1 Melt the butter in a large flameproof casserole or cast-iron pan over a moderate heat, brown the pheasant all over, then transfer the bird to a plate. Reduce the heat, add the bacon, and cook for 1 minute. Add the onion, celery, and carrot, and cook until the onion has softened.

2 Return the pheasant to the pan and add the sage, Marsala, and stock. Season with salt and pepper, bring to a boil, cover, and simmer gently for 35–40 minutes, adding the chestnuts after 20–25 minutes. Or if you prefer, cook in a preheated oven, 325°F.

3 To make the beet straws, peel the beets and slice into very thin rounds, then cut the rounds into very fine julienne strips. Place on paper towels, and leave to dry out for 30 minutes. Pat dry well. Heat the oil to 350–375°F, or until a cube of bread browns in 30 seconds. Cook the beet strips in batches until crisp, then drain on paper towels.

4 Remove the pheasant from the casserole, and keep warm. Skim off any excess fat from the surface. Place the casserole over the heat, and boil rapidly until the sauce reduces and thickens slightly. Adjust the seasoning, then serve the sauce with the pheasant, accompanied by the beet straws.

2 tablespoons butter

1 pheasant, about 2–2¼ lb.

¼ lb. pancetta or regular bacon, cut into strips

1 large onion, chopped

1 celery stalk, chopped

1 large carrot, chopped

1 tablespoon chopped sage

½ cup Marsala

2 cups chicken stock

8 oz. vacuum-packed cooked chestnuts (around 3½ cups)

salt and pepper

Beet Straws:

½ lb. raw beets

oil, for deep-frying

Serves 4

Preparation time: 30 minutes plus drying the beet straws

Cooking time: 1–1½ hours

chicken with artichokes

1 To prepare the artichokes, remove the hard outer leaves, then peel back the center leaves so you can cut out each choke. With a sharp knife, remove the stems of the artichokes. Have ready a large bowl of water and add the lemon juice. Immerse the prepared artichokes in this acidulated water for at least 30 minutes. Remove and drain.

2 Heat the oil in a large sauté or frying pan, and gently fry the artichokes and small onions for about 15 minutes, until golden. Add the chicken breasts to the pan, and fry for a few minutes on each side, until golden brown. Add the garlic, herbs, and wine, and cook over a low heat for 10–15 minutes, or until the chicken is cooked through.

3 Remove the chicken, artichokes, and onions, and keep warm. Increase the heat and boil the pan juices, scraping the bottom of the pan with a wooden spoon to lift all the deposits, until thickened and reduced. Season to taste and pour the sauce over the chicken. Garnish with the parsley and serve at once.

8 small young artichokes

¼ cup lemon juice

⅓ cup olive oil

½ lb. pearl onions, peeled

4 boneless, skinless chicken breasts

3 garlic cloves

thyme sprigs

1 bay leaf

a scant cup dry white wine

salt and pepper

2 tablespoons chopped flat-leaf parsley, to garnish

Serves 4

Preparation time: 15 minutes plus soaking

Cooking time: 35–40 minutes

■ Soaking the artichokes, or any other vegetable or fruit, in acidulated water helps to prevent discoloration.

tandoori chicken

1 Trim the chicken, leaving the skin on, and make three slashes on each thigh. Arrange the thighs in a single layer in a non-metallic dish. Combine the yogurt and tandoori paste, and coat the chicken. Cover and leave to marinate for 30 minutes.

2 Heat the butter or ghee in a large, heavy-based pan. Add the ginger and onion, and cook until golden. Stir in the mint and cilantro, and cook for 30 seconds, then remove the mixture and set aside.

3 Add the garlic, ground coriander, and cumin to the pan and cook over medium heat for 1 minute. Add the chicken thighs, in batches if necessary, and cook on each side for 3 minutes. Return all the thighs to the pan, skin side up, add the stock, and bring slowly to a boil. Reduce the heat, cover, and simmer for 25 minutes. Remove the lid and cook for a further 10–12 minutes.

4 Spoon the onion mixture over the chicken, and cook for about 1 minute until hot. Serve with a spoonful of the sauce and lemon or lime wedges.

■ To make pure ghee, melt 2 sticks (1 cup) butter in a saucepan, and simmer for 10-12 minutes. When the froth turns golden, strain. Store in a jar.

6 chicken thighs or other pieces

¼ cup plain yogurt

¼ cup tandoori paste

2 tablespoons butter or ghee

2-inch piece fresh ginger, peeled and cut into thin strips

1 red onion, cut into thin wedges

¾–1 cup chopped mint

¾–1 cup chopped cilantro

2 garlic cloves, chopped

1 teaspoon ground coriander

1 teapoon ground cumin

¾ cup chicken stock

lemon or lime wedges, to garnish

Serves 4

Preparation time: 10 minutes plus marinating

Cooking time: about 45 minutes

1½ teaspoons coriander seeds

1½ teaspoons cumin seeds

¼ teaspoon black onion seeds

¼ teaspoon fenugreek seeds

¼ teaspoon mustard seeds

1-inch piece cinnamon stick

3 cloves

¾ teaspoon peppercorns

2 tablespoons dried coconut

2 tablespoons unsalted peanuts

6 tablespoons vinegar

2 garlic cloves, crushed

1 teaspoon chopped fresh ginger

½ teaspoon ground turmeric

1½ teaspoons ground red pepper

2 teaspoons salt

3 lb. chicken, skinned and cut into pieces

3 tablespoons vegetable oil

12 curry leaves plus extra, to garnish

1 teaspoon cumin seeds

fried onion rings, to garnish

1 Dry-roast the coriander, cumin, black onion, fenugreek, mustard, cinnamon, cloves, peppercorns, coconut, and peanuts, then grind them in a spice grinder. Transfer to a bowl, then mix in the vinegar, garlic, ginger, turmeric, ground red pepper, and salt. Spread the mixture over the chicken pieces, cover, and marinate overnight in the refrigerator.

2 Heat the oil in a wok, then add the curry leaves and cumin seeds. Cook for a further 10 seconds, then add the chicken and cook for 15 minutes, turning once or twice. Cover and cook for a further 15–20 minutes or until the chicken is tender, adding a little water from time to time to keep the chicken moist. Leave over a very low heat for a few minutes before serving, garnished with the onion rings and some shredded curry leaves.

Serves 4–6

Preparation time: 20 minutes plus marinating

Cooking time: 30–40 minutes

chicken vindaloo

spicy duck in port with fresh figs

1 Place the duck in a large bowl, add the marinade ingredients, stir well, cover, and marinate in the refrigerator for at least 2 hours or overnight.

2 Remove the duck from the marinade, reserving the marinade, and pat dry. Heat a large flameproof casserole or cast-iron pan over medium heat, add the duck, in batches, skin side down first, and brown all over. Transfer each batch to a colander to drain. Pour off most of the fat that has been rendered from the duck, leaving about 1 tablespoon.

3 Add the onion and garlic to the casserole and cook gently for 5 minutes until softened. Return the duck pieces, pour in the marinade, bring to a boil, and add the stock. Bring back to a boil, reduce the heat, and season. Cover with a tight-fitting lid and simmer for 45 minutes. Remove the lid, skim off any fat, and lay the figs on top. Cover and cook for a further 20–30 minutes, or until the meat and figs are tender.

4 Remove the meat and figs from the casserole and keep warm. Discard the star anise, cinnamon, bay leaf, and thyme. Skim off as much fat as possible. Increase the heat and boil rapidly until the sauce is reduced by half. Serve the duck with the sauce spooned over it.

4 lb. duck, cut into 8 pieces

1 onion, chopped

1–2 garlic cloves, crushed

2 cups chicken stock

12 ripe figs

salt and pepper

Marinade:

1¾ cups port

4 whole star anise

2-inch piece cinnamon stick

4 cloves

8 Szechuan or black peppercorns

2 tablespoons chopped stem ginger

¼ cup honey

1 piece orange or tangerine peel

1 bay leaf

1 thyme sprig

Serves 4

Preparation time: 30 minutes plus marinating

Cooking time: 1½ hours

roast pheasant flambéed with calvados

1 Place the pheasant in a roasting pan. Tuck the onion halves under the bird, and sprinkle with a little salt and pepper. Dot with the butter, place in a preheated oven, 375°F, and roast for about 45 minutes, or until the pheasant is cooked through and tender, adding the apples 15–20 minutes before the end of the cooking.

2 Transfer the pheasant to a warmed serving dish. Place the apple slices in a separate dish, and keep them hot while making the sauce.

3 Stir the flour into the pan juices, and cook over a moderate heat for 1 minute. Stir in the wine and bring to a boil, stirring all the time. Remove from the heat. Heat the Calvados in a small saucepan until it is just warm, then ignite it and, when the flames die down, add it to the sauce. Stir in the heavy cream and chopped parsley. Taste for seasoning, then reheat the sauce without boiling.

4 Pour a little of the sauce around the pheasant, and arrange the apples in the dish. Serve with roasted potatoes and vegetables, with the remaining sauce served separately.

1 oven-ready pheasant, preferably a hen bird

1 small onion, cut in half

2 tablespoons butter

2 tart eating apples, peeled, cored, and thickly sliced

salt and pepper

Sauce:

1 tablespoon all-purpose flour

⅔ cup dry white wine

2 tablespoons Calvados or apple jack

¼ cup heavy cream

1 tablespoon chopped parsley

salt and pepper

Serves 2
Preparation time: 20 minutes
Cooking time: 45 minutes

chicken in red wine

1 Heat the oil and butter in a large, heavy pan and add the chicken pieces. Fry over low heat until golden on all sides, turning occasionally. Remove the chicken from the pan with a slotted spoon, and keep warm. Pour off a little of the fat, then add the pearl onions and bacon, and fry until lightly colored, then sprinkle in the flour and stir well.

2 Pour in the wine and bring to a boil, stirring. Add the bouquet garni, unpeeled garlic cloves, sugar, nutmeg, and salt and pepper to taste. Return the chicken to the pan, lower the heat, cover, and simmer for 15 minutes.

3 Add the mushrooms and cook gently for a further 45 minutes, or until the chicken pieces are cooked and just tender. Remove with a slotted spoon and arrange on a warmed serving plate. Keep hot. Pour the brandy into the sauce and boil, uncovered, for 15 minutes, or until thick and reduced. Remove and discard the bouquet garni and garlic cloves.

4 Pour the sauce over the chicken and garnish with chopped parsley. Serve with some fried bread triangles to mop up the sauce, if you like.

2 tablespoons oil

½ stick (¼ cup) butter

5 lb. chicken, cut into 12 pieces

24 small pearl onions, peeled

¼ lb. slice smoked ham, diced

1 tablespoon all-purpose flour

1 bottle Burgundy or other good red wine

1 bouquet garni

2 garlic cloves, unpeeled

pinch of sugar

freshly grated nutmeg

24 button mushrooms

1 tablespoon brandy

salt and pepper

2 tablespoons finely chopped parsley, to garnish

fried bread triangles, to serve (optional)

Serves 6–8

Preparation time: 15–20 minutes

Cooking time: 1½ hours

burgundy-style beef

1 Put a few onion slices in a deep bowl with a little parsley, thyme, and some crumbled bay leaf. Place a few pieces of beef on top, and continue layering up in this way, until all the onion, beef, and herbs are used up. Mix the brandy with the wine and oil, and pour over the beef. Cover, and marinate in the refrigerator for at least 4 hours.

2 Melt the butter in a flameproof casserole or cast-iron pan, add the bacon and fry over a moderate heat until golden brown. Remove and set aside. Add the small onions and fry until golden all over. Remove and set aside. Add the mushrooms and fry, stirring, for about 1 minute. Drain and set aside.

3 Remove the beef from the marinade, then strain the marinade and set aside. Add the beef to the casserole and fry briskly until browned. Sprinkle in the flour and cook, stirring, for 1 minute. Gradually stir in the strained marinade, then add the stock, garlic, and bouquet garni. Season to taste, cover, and simmer gently for 2 hours.

4 Skim off any fat on the surface, and add the bacon, onions, and mushrooms to the casserole. Cover and simmer for 30 minutes, or until the beef is tender. Discard the bouquet garni and serve immediately.

1 large onion, thinly sliced

a few parsley sprigs

a few thyme sprigs

1 bay leaf, crushed

2 lb. chuck steak or sirloin, cut into chunks

2 tablespoons brandy

1¾ cups red Burgundy or other good red wine

2 tablespoons olive oil

½ stick (¼ cup) butter

5 oz. lean bacon (around 5–6 strips), roughly chopped

24 small pearl onions, peeled

1 lb. button mushrooms, cut in half (around 6 cups)

¼ cup all-purpose flour

1¼ cups beef or chicken stock

1 garlic clove, crushed

1 bouquet garni

salt and pepper

Serves 4–6

Preparation time: 30 minutes plus marinating

Cooking time: 2½ hours

beef & new potato salad

1 Cook the pepper halves, skin side up, under a preheated hot broiler for about 10–15 minutes, without turning, until the skin is blackened and blistered all over. Transfer to a bowl, cover with paper towles, and set aside, then rub off and discard the charred skin; cut the flesh into strips. Set aside.

2 Season the beef with pepper. Broil for about 5 minutes, turning once, until well browned on the outside but still rare on the inside. Transfer to a plate and leave to cool.

3 Cut the potatoes in half. Place in a bowl with the pepper strips, green beans, onion, tomatoes, and olives. Slice the beef thinly, cutting across the grain, and add to the bowl with the thyme. Season with salt and pepper to taste.

4 Combine all the ingredients for the dressing in a screw-top jar, and shake well. Spoon it over the salad and toss lightly.

1 red bell pepper, cut in half, cored, and seeded

¾ lb. beef tenderloin, cut into 1-inch steaks

1 lb. small new potatoes, boiled and cooled

¼ lb. (around ¾ cup) green beans, cooked and cooled

½ red onion, thinly sliced

⅔ cup red and yellow cherry tomatoes, cut in half

about 16 anchovy-stuffed green olives

a few black olives (optional)

2 teaspoons chopped thyme

salt and pepper

Sweet Mustard Dressing:

3 tablespoons olive oil

2 tablespoons whole-grain mustard

1 tablespoon honey

1 teaspoon lemon juice

Serves 4–6

Preparation time: 30 minutes

Cooking time: about 25 minutes

lamb & apricot tagine

1 Place the meat in a large flameproof casserole and add the onion, garlic, all the spices, and lemon zest and juice. Mix well and add the water to cover. Bring to a boil, then reduce the heat, cover the casserole, and simmer for 1 hour.

2 Stir in the honey, apricots, and parsley, season with salt and pepper to taste, and cook, covered, for a further 30 minutes until the lamb is tender.

3 Meanwhile, heat the oil in a frying pan, add the almonds, and cook, shaking the pan occasionally, for 5 minutes, or until evenly golden.

4 When the meat is cooked, if the sauce is too thin, remove the meat with a slotted spoon and keep it warm while you boil the sauce, uncovered, until it reduces to the right consistency. Sprinkle the tagine with the almonds, and serve with couscous or rice.

2 lb. boneless lean lamb, trimmed and cut into 1-inch cubes

1 large onion, chopped

2 garlic cloves, crushed

1 teaspoon ground coriander

1 teaspoon ground cumin

½ teaspoon ground cinnamon

¼ teaspoon ground ginger

pinch of saffron threads

2 thin strips lemon zest

2 tablespoons fresh lemon juice

2½–4 cups water

1–2 tablespoons honey

1¼–1½ cups dried apricots, soaked in warm water for 15 minutes

1 tablespoon chopped flat-leaf parsley

1 tablespoon olive oil

½ cup whole blanched almonds

salt and pepper

Serves 4

Preparation time: 20 minutes plus soaking

Cooking time: 1½ hours

12 noisettes of lamb or lamb cutlets

1 pomegranate, cut in half

3 scallions, finely chopped

½ teaspoon black peppercorns, lightly crushed

⅔ cup lamb or beef stock

⅔ cup red wine

parsley sprigs, to garnish

noisettes of lamb with pomegranate

Serves 6

Preparation time: 15 minutes plus marinating

Cooking time: about 20 minutes

1 Trim any excess fat from the noisettes and put them in a shallow dish, in one layer. Using a lemon squeezer, squeeze the juice from the pomegranate and pour it over the lamb. Add the scallions and peppercorns. Cover and marinate in the refrigerator for at least 2 hours. Drain the noisettes, reserving the marinade, and dry them on paper towels.

2 In a non-stick pan, fry the lamb noisettes without added fat, to seal them on both sides. Pour over them the stock and red wine. Simmer, uncovered, until the liquid has reduced by about half. Add the reserved marinade and bring to a boil.

3 Remove the noisettes from the pan with a slotted spoon, and arrange them on a warmed serving plate. Garnish with parsley sprigs. Pour the sauce over them and serve with new potatoes and a green vegetable.

■ Pomegranates are usually only available for a limited season during the winter months, but they are excellent served with some of the richer meats, and help to tenderize the flesh, too.

1 Heat half the butter and the oil in a frying pan, and gently cook the onion and garlic until soft. Add the mushrooms and nutmeg, and season with salt and pepper. Stir over a gentle heat until the mushrooms are cooked and the moisture has evaporated. Remove from the pan, divide into 4 portions, and leave to cool.

2 Heat the remaining butter in a clean frying pan, add the tenderloin steaks, and sear quickly on both sides. Remove from the pan, cool quickly, and keep chilled until needed.

3 Roll out the pastry on a lightly floured surface, and cut into 4 circles large enough to half-cover the steaks. Brush a 1-inch border around the edge of each circle with beaten egg. Cut the ham into 4 circles the same size as the steaks.

4 Place 1 piece of ham on each of 2 pastry circles. Cover the ham with a portion of the mushroom mixture, a tenderloin steak, another portion of mushrooms, and another circle of ham. Top with a pastry circle. Seal the edges of the pastry between your fingers and then press with a fork. Cut any pastry trimmings into leaves, and use these to decorate the croûtes. Brush with beaten egg, and cook in a preheated oven, 425°F, for 20 minutes, until golden brown. Serve with new potatoes and asparagus.

2 tablespoons butter

1 tablespoon oil

1 small onion, finely chopped

1 garlic clove, crushed

a generous ½ cup finely chopped mushrooms

pinch of grated nutmeg

2 beef tenderloin steaks, about 6 oz. each, trimmed

4 oz. fresh or frozen puff pastry, defrosted

1 egg, beaten

2 slices ham

salt and pepper

Serves 2

Preparation time: 20 minutes

Cooking time: 30–35 minutes

tournedos en croûte

tenderloin steak with smoked oysters

1 Carefully cut three-quarters of the way through each steak, and open out butterfly-style. Place between 2 sheets of wax paper, and beat with a rolling pin to an even thickness.

2 Season with salt and pepper, and brush lightly with a little oil. Place under a preheated hot broiler and cook for 6–10 minutes.

3 Meanwhile, heat the remaining oil in a pan and sauté the onions and mushrooms for about 5 minutes or until soft. Add the wine, stock, and tomato paste, and simmer for about 3–4 minutes, until the liquid is slightly reduced and thickened. Add the drained oysters.

4 Spoon the sauce over the steaks and garnish with watercress.

10 oz. beef tenderloin, cut into 2 steaks

1 tablespoon vegetable oil

⅓ cup finely sliced onions

¾ cup finely sliced button mushrooms

2 tablespoons red wine

2 tablespoons beef or chicken stock

1 tablespoon tomato paste

5–6 canned smoked oysters, drained

salt and pepper

watercress, to garnish

Serves 2
Preparation time: 15 minutes
Cooking time: 15–20 minutes

roghan ghosht

1 Heat 2 tablespoons of the oil in a large pan, add half of the onions, and fry until golden. Add the lamb and ¾ cup of the yogurt, stir well, then cover and simmer for 20 minutes.

2 Meanwhile, put the garlic, ginger, chiles, coriander seeds, cumin seeds, mint, cilantro, and 2–3 tablespoons of the yogurt in a food processor or blender and work to a smooth paste.

3 Heat the remaining oil in a large pan, add the cardamom, cloves, and cinnamon, and fry quickly for 1 minute, stirring. Add the remaining onion and the prepared spice paste, and fry for 5 minutes, stirring constantly. Add the lamb and yogurt mixture, season to taste, stir well, and bring to a simmering point. Cover and cook for 30 minutes.

4 Add the almonds and cook for a further 15 minutes, until the meat is tender. Remove the whole spices before serving. Garnish with fried onion rings and lemon slices, and serve immediately.

¼ cup oil

2 onions, finely chopped

1½ lb. boned leg of lamb, cubed

1¼ cups plain yogurt

2 garlic cloves

1-inch piece fresh ginger, peeled and roughly chopped

2 green chiles, seeded

1 tablespoon coriander seeds

1 teaspoon cumin seeds

1 teaspoon chopped mint leaves

1 teaspoon chopped cilantro

6 cardamom pods, crushed

6 cloves

1-inch piece cinnamon stick

¾–1 cup sliced almonds

salt and pepper

To Garnish:

fried onion rings

lemon slices

Serves 4

Preparation time: 20 minutes

Cooking time: about 1¼ hours

ginger cake ●

tarte tatin ●

champagne summer berries ●

chocolate & cinnamon bread & butter pudding ●

chocolate truffles ●

chocolate & orange roulade ●

chocolate chip ice cream ●

exotic fruit salad ●

lemon tart ●

red fruit salad with coeurs à la crème ●

desserts

ginger cake

1 Line and grease a 7-inch cake pan. Cream the butter and sugar together in a mixing bowl, until light and fluffy. Add the eggs one at a time, adding a tablespoon of flour with the last two eggs. Sift and fold in the remaining flour and the ground ginger, then fold in the preserved ginger and syrup.

2 Pour the mixture into the prepared cake pan and bake in a preheated oven, 350°F, for 1–1½ hours. Tip out onto a wire rack to cool.

3 To make the ginger icing, beat the confectioners' sugar and syrup together until smooth. Pour the icing over the cake and leave until set. Decorate the cake with ginger strips.

1½ sticks (¾ cup) butter

¾ cup superfine or regular sugar

3 eggs

2 cups self-rising flour

½ teaspoon ground ginger

⅔ cup chopped preserved ginger

2 tablespoons ginger syrup

preserved ginger strips, to decorate

Ginger Icing:

1⅓ cups confectioners' sugar, sifted

2 tablespoons ginger syrup

Makes one 7-inch cake
Preparation time: 15 minutes
Cooking time: 1–1½ hours

tarte tatin

1   Place the flour in a bowl, add the diced butter, and rub in with your fingertips until the mixture resembles fine breadcrumbs. Stir in the sugar. Add the egg yolk and enough water, about 2–3 tablespoons, to mix to a firm and smooth dough.

2   To prepare the apple mixture, melt the butter and sugar in an 8-inch ovenproof frying pan. When the mixture is golden, add the apples and toss them in the syrup to coat them. Cook for a few minutes, until the apples start to caramelize.

3   Roll out the dough on a lightly floured surface to a circle, a little larger than the pan. Place it over the apples, folding over the edges of the dough until it fits the pan neatly.

4   Bake in a preheated oven, 400°F, for 35–40 minutes, or until the crust is golden. Cool in the pan for 5 minutes, place a large plate on top of the pan and invert the tart onto it. Serve warm with thick cream, served separately, if you like.

thick cream, to serve

Pastry Dough:

1½ cups all-purpose flour

¾ stick (⅓ cup) chilled butter, diced

2 tablespoons sugar

1 egg yolk

Apple Mixture:

½ stick (¼ cup) butter

¼ cup sugar

6 eating apples, peeled, cored, and quartered

Serves 4–6
Preparation time: 20 minutes
Cooking time: 35–40 minutes

■ A delicious variation is to substitute the apples with 5 pears, and sprinkle with ½ cup walnut halves before covering with the pastry. Then follow the main recipe.

champagne summer berries

1 Mix all the berries in a ceramic bowl and sprinkle them with half of the sugar and half of the lemon juice. Set aside for 10 minutes.

2 Meanwhile, pour the remaining sugar onto a large plate. Dip the rims of four glass dessert bowls into the remaining lemon juice, shake off the excess, then dip each bowl into the sugar. The sugar will cling to the lemon juice, making an attractive frosted rim.

3 Cover the bowls with aluminum foil, and tie it down. Place in a steamer, or in a covered pan half-filled with boiling water, and steam for about 3–5 minutes.

4 To serve, spoon the fruit into the prepared bowls, being careful not to spoil the frosted rims. At the table, pour the chilled champagne over the fruit, and decorate with mint sprigs. Serve with almond cookies.

1 cup strawberries, hulled and cut in half

1 cup raspberries

½ cup red currants, topped and tailed

½ cup blueberries

2 tablespoons sugar

¼ cup lemon juice

1 cup chilled champagne

mint sprigs, to decorate

almond cookies, to serve

Serves 4
Preparation time: 15 minutes plus marinating
Cooking time: 3–5 minutes

1 Spread the sliced bread with the butter, and sprinkle with the cinnamon. Cut each slice of bread into 4 triangles.

2 Beat the sugar and eggs together in a bowl. Heat the milk, coffee, and half of the chocolate, to just above room temperature. Whisk until well blended, then pour it over the eggs. Mix well.

3 Layer the bread slices in a lightly greased deep pie dish (or 1 qt.-casserole), and strain the custard over it. Set aside for at least 30 minutes.

4 Place the dish in a water bath, pour about 1 quart of water around the dish, and bake at 350°F for 1¼–1½ hours, or until the custard is set. About 10 minutes before the end of cooking time, sprinkle the remaining chocolate over it.

4 large slices white bread, crusts removed

2 tablespoons butter, softened

1 teaspoon ground cinnamon

3 tablespoons sugar

3 eggs

2½ cups milk

1 teaspoon instant coffee powder or granules

1 cup grated dark chocolate

Serves 2

Preparation time: 10 minutes plus standing

Cooking time: 1¼–1½ hours

chocolate & cinnamon bread & butter pudding

chocolate truffles

1   Heat the cream gently until tepid. Put half of the chocolate pieces into a small bowl and melt gently over hot, but not boiling, water, stirring occasionally. Do not rest the base of the bowl in the hot water. Remove the bowl from the heat and slowly pour in the cream, stirring thoroughly.

2   Set the mixture aside to cool, then add the whiskey or brandy. Whisk for 3–4 minutes, or until the mixture is light and stands in peaks. Chill in the refrigerator for about 20 minutes.

3   Sift the cocoa powder onto a tray. Roll spoonfuls of the chocolate paste into balls about 1 inch in diameter, then roll them in the cocoa powder to cover. Leave to cool until firm.

4   To cover the truffles in chocolate, melt the remaining chocolate over hot water. Spear each truffle on a skewer, and dip them one by one into the melted chocolate. Place on a marble slab or foil to set. Dust with the cocoa powder to serve.

3 tablespoons heavy cream

9 oz. bittersweet or semi-sweet chocolate, broken into small pieces (around 1½–1¾ cups)

½–1 tablespoon whiskey or brandy (optional)

2 tablespoons cocoa powder, for dusting

Makes 10 truffles

Preparation time: 40 minutes plus chilling

chocolate & orange roulade

1 In a mixing bowl, whisk the egg yolks and sugar until thick and creamy. Sift the cocoa powder over the mixture and fold in thoroughly. In a second bowl, whisk the egg whites until stiff, and gently fold into the chocolate mixture.

2 Spoon into a greased and lined 12 x 8-inch baking sheet with sides, and level the surface. Bake in a preheated oven, 350°F, for 25–30 minutes, or until firm. Cool for 5 minutes, then cover with a damp towel, and leave until completely cold.

3 Sift the confectioners' sugar over a large sheet of wax paper. Invert the cake onto the wax paper, and carefully peel off the lining paper.

4 Put the cream into a bowl and whip until thick. Add the sour cream, confectioners' sugar, orange zest and liqueur. Mix gently. Spread the mixture over the cake, then roll it up like a jelly roll, with the help of the wax paper. Transfer the roulade to a serving dish and dust with more confectioners' sugar if you like. Serve immediately. The cake may crack when rolled but this is quite normal.

4 eggs, separated

¾ cup superfine or regular sugar

⅓ cup cocoa powder

confectioners' sugar, sifted

Filling:

⅔ cup heavy cream

⅔ cup sour cream

2 tablespoons confectioners' sugar, sifted

finely grated zest of 1 orange

1 tablespoon orange liqueur

Serves 6–8
Preparation time: 30 minutes plus cooling
Cooking time: 25–30 minutes

chocolate chip ice cream

1 Whip the cream with the sugar until it holds its shape on the whisk. Transfer to a freezer tray or a lidded container so that it can be beaten easily. Freeze the cream for 30 minutes, beat thoroughly, then freeze again for a further 30 minutes.

2 Meanwhile, spread the breadcrumbs on a broiler pan, and sprinkle with the brown sugar. Place under a preheated broiler until the sugar caramelizes. Stir well to ensure even browning. Leave to cool.

3 If necessary, grind or crush the breadcrumbs to break up any lumps. Stir in the hazelnuts.

4 Remove the frozen cream from the freezer, and beat thoroughly. Stir in the breadcrumb mixture, then the chopped chocolate. Mix well, then return to the freezer for a further 2 hours, after which it is ready to eat. Anytime the ice cream has been frozen for 24 hours or more, be sure to allow it to soften for 1 hour before serving.

2½ cups heavy cream

1 tablespoon sugar

4 cups fresh whole-wheat breadcrumbs

a scant ½ cup soft dark brown sugar

½ cup hazelnuts, chopped and toasted

4 squares unsweetened or semi-sweet baking chocolate, chopped

Makes 1¼ pints

Preparation time: about 20 minutes plus freezing

■ Turn your freezer to the fast-freeze setting before starting to make this recipe, but don't forget to turn it back to the usual setting afterward.

1 Cut the top off the pineapple, and pull away 2 or 3 leaves. Cut the pineapple in half lengthwise, and cut out the flesh of the pineapple by cutting around it with a long, sharp knife, and scooping out the flesh with a spoon. Slice the flesh into bite-size pieces, discarding the core.

2 Cut the passion fruit in half, and spoon out the flesh.

3 Mix all the fruits together in a bowl with the kirsch. Spoon them into the pineapple shell and chill.

4 Just before serving, decorate with the pineapple leaves. Serve with yogurt, or half & half, or light cream.

1 small pineapple

1 passion fruit

1 kiwi fruit, peeled and sliced

1 mango, peeled and sliced, pit removed

3 tablespoons kirsch

plain yogurt or half & half or light cream, to serve

Serves 2

Preparation time: 30 minutes plus cooling

exotic fruit salad

■ To speed up the ripening process of unripe kiwis, place them in a plastic bag with a ripe apple or pear.

lemon tart

1 To make the pastry, sift the flour and salt into a bowl and rub in the butter until the mixture resembles breadcrumbs. Stir in the egg yolk and enough iced water to make a soft and pliable dough. Chill in the refrigerator for 30 minutes.

2 To make the filling, put the lemon zest and juice, and sugar, in a mixing bowl. Add the eggs and add the egg white and beat well. Then beat in the cream, ground almonds, and cinnamon. The mixture should be thick and smooth.

3 Roll out the dough on a lightly floured surface, and use to line a 10-inch removable-bottomed fluted tart pan. Prick the base with a fork and pour in the filling mixture. Bake in a preheated oven, 375°F, for 20 minutes, or until it is set and golden. Set aside to cool.

4 To make the topping, heat the lemon slices in a little water over low heat for about 10 minutes, or until tender. Remove and drain the lemon slices, keeping about 3 oz. of the liquid. Add the sugar and stir over gentle heat until dissolved. Bring to a boil, add the lemon slices, and cook rapidly until they are coated with thick syrup. Remove and use them to decorate the tart. Leave to cool and serve.

2 cups all-purpose flour

pinch of salt

1 stick (½ cup) butter

1 egg yolk

2–3 tablespoons ice water

Filling:

grated zest and juice of 3 lemons

⅓ cup sugar

2 eggs plus 1 egg white

⅓ cup heavy cream

1¼ cups ground almonds

a good pinch of ground cinnamon

Topping:

2 lemons, thinly sliced

½ cup superfine or regular sugar

Serves 6–8

Preparation time: 15 minutes plus chilling

Cooking time: 30 minutes

red fruit salad with coeurs à la crème

1 First make the coeurs à la crème. Sprinkle the gelatin on the water in a small bowl. Stir well, then stand the bowl in hot water to dissolve.

2 Beat together the cottage cheese, yogurt, and cream, then stir in the dissolved gelatin. Spoon the mixture into 2 heart-shaped draining molds. Leave overnight.

3 Put half of the raspberries in a food processor and blend to a purée, then press through a strainer. Stir the honey into the purée over a low heat. Stir in the remaining raspberries, the cherries, and black currants, and simmer gently for 2–3 minutes. Leave to cool, then chill in the refrigerator for at least 1 hour.

4 Gently tip out the molds and decorate them with a pinch of grated nutmeg. Serve with the red fruit salad arranged around the heart.

around 2¼ cups raspberries

2 tablespoons honey

¾ cup sweet cherries, pitted

½ cup black currants or blueberries

Coeurs à la Crème:

1 teaspoon granulated gelatin

1 tablespoon hot water

¾ cup cottage cheese, strained

⅓ cup plain yogurt

2 tablespoons heavy cream

grated nutmeg

Serves 2

Preparation time: 30 minutes plus overnight draining and chilling

Cooking time: 5 minutes

index

apples: tarte tatin 85
asparagus: crab, asparagus & lemon soup 20
   lobster & asparagus salad 34
avocado, prosciutto with 12

beef: beef & new potato salad 75
   Burgundy-style beef 74
   tenderloin steak with smoked oysters 80
   tournedos en croûte 78
bread & butter pudding, chocolate 88
Burgundy-style beef 74

Camembert & cranberry pie 57
champagne summer berries 86
cheese: Camembert & cranberry pie 57
chicken: chicken in red wine 73
   chicken vindaloo 68
   classic paella 31
   tandoori chicken 67
   with artichokes 66
chocolate: chocolate & cinnamon bread & butter
      pudding 88
   chocolate & orange roulade 90
   chocolate chip ice cream 91
   chocolate truffles 89
cod: Thai steamed fish curry 45
coeurs à la crème 95
crab: crab, asparagus & lemon soup 20
   dressed crab 19
curries 45, 68, 81

duck: spicy duck in port with fresh figs 70
   with orange 64

eggplants with tomatoes 52

fruit: champagne summer berries 86
   exotic fruit salad 93
   red fruit salad with coeurs à la crème 95

ginger cake 84
globe artichokes with garlic & herb
      mayonnaise 27

guinea fowl with fresh gnocchi 63

ice cream, chocolate chip 91

lamb: lamb & apricot tagine 76
   noisettes with pomegranate 77
   roghan ghosht 81
leek terrine with walnuts & feta 53
lemon tart 94
lobster: lobster & asparagus salad 34
   lobster thermidor 37

mayonnaise 9
Mediterranean vegetable salad 51
monkfish & vegetable parcels 36
mushrooms: spinach & mushroom roulade 50
   tagliatelle with cream & 58
   wild mushroom feuilleté 15
   wild mushroom salad with croûtons 59

wild mushrooms in crispy cases 55
mussels: classic paella 31
   mussels in white wine sauce 32
   Normandy-style sole 43

Normandy-style sole 43

oysters: tenderloin steak with smoked oysters 80
   oysters in cream sauce 18
   smoked oyster tartlets 22

paella, classic 31
pears wrapped in prosciutto 17
pheasant: braised with Marsala & chestnuts 65
   roast pheasant flambéed with Calvados 71
potatoes: beef & new potato salad 75
prosciutto: pears wrapped in 17
   with avocado 12

quail egg tartlets 14

rice: classic paella 31
   seafood risotto 41
roghan ghosht 81

salads 34, 51, 59, 75
salmon: pan-fried with tomato coulis 33
   seviche of salmon 16
   with three sauces 44
seafood risotto 41
shrimp: Thai shrimp parcels 26
   Thai tomato & shrimp broth 25
skate in orange & cider sauce 39
smoked salmon timbales 23
sole: Normandy-style sole 43
   sole bonne femme 42
soups 20, 25
spinach & mushroom roulade 50
squid: classic paella 31

tagliatelle with mushrooms & cream 58
tandoori chicken 67
taramasalata: smoked salmon timbales 23
tarte tatin 85
Thai shrimp parcels 26
Thai steamed fish curry 45
Thai tomato & shrimp broth 25
tomatoes: pan-fried salmon with 33
   spicy eggplants with 52
   Thai tomato & shrimp broth 25
tournedos en croûte 78
trout with almonds 38

vegetables: in Malaysian coconut sauce 48
   seasonal vegetable medley 54
   vegetable terrine 56